Mysteries OF THE Rain Forest

20th Century Medicine Man

Produced in cooperation with

WTTW Chicago

and

Kurtis Productions, Ltd.

Adapted by
Elaine Pascoe

 A BLACKBIRCH PRESS BOOK
WOODBRIDGE, CONNECTICUT

Published by Blackbirch Press, Inc.
260 Amity Road
Woodbridge, CT 06525

web site: http://www.blackbirch.com
email: staff@blackbirch.com

For WTTW Chicago
Edward Menaker, Executive Producer
For Kurtis Productions, Ltd.
Bill Kurtis, Executive Producer

©1998 Blackbirch Press, Inc.
First Edition

Printed in the United States of America

10 9 8 7 6 5 4 3 2 1

Library of Congress Cataloging-in-Publication Data

Pascoe, Elaine.
    Mysteries of the rain forest : 20th century medicine man / by Elaine Pascoe.
        p.   cm. — (New explorers)
    Includes bibliographical references and index.
    Summary: Describes the experiences of an ethnobotanist in South America as he learns from Tirío Indians the medicinal value of rain forest plants, and struggles to record the data before these ancient traditions vanish.
    ISBN 1-56711-229-3 (lib. bdg. : alk. paper)
    1. Tirío Indians—Ethnobotany—Juvenile literature. 2. Plotkin, Mark J.—Juvenile literature. 3. Ethnobotany—Surinam—Juvenile literature. 4. Ethnobotany—Amazon River Valley—Juvenile literature. 5. Traditional medicine—Surinam—Juvenile literature. 6. Traditional medicine—Amazon River Valley—Juvenile literature.
[1. Ethnobotany—Amazon River Valley. 2. Tirío Indians. 3. Indians of South American—Amazon River Valley. 4. Plotkin, Mark J. 5. Traditional medicine] I. Title. II. Series.
F2420.1.T7P37   1998
581.6'34'089984—dc21   94-49616
                                                                                           CIP
                                                                                            AC

INTRODUCTION

In 1990, I was lucky enough to help create a very special new "club." Its members come from all corners of the earth and are of all ages. They can be found braving crowded cities, floating among brilliantly colored coral reefs, and scaling desolate mountaintops. We call these people "New Explorers" because—in one way or another—they seek to uncover important knowledge or travel to places that others merely dream of.

No matter where they are, or what they do, New Explorers dedicate their lives to expanding the horizons of their science. Some are biologists. Others are physicists, neurosurgeons, or ethnobotanists. Still others are engineers, teachers, even cave divers. Each of them has worked hard to push limits—to go the extra step in the pursuit of a truly significant discovery.

In his quest for a breakthrough, Mike Madden is a typical New Explorer. For eight years, he was obsessed with proving that a 27-mile (44-kilometer) underwater cave system was actually connected to the Caribbean Sea. To do this, Madden swam through tunnels never before traveled by humans. Each dive was a calculated risk—a very great one—but well worth it, for Madden also proved this was the longest underwater cave system in the world.

Madden's story, like those of all the New Explorers, is what science is all about. Science is about adventure. It's about curiosity and discovery. And, sometimes, science is also about danger.

New Explorers make it clear that science is not confined to laboratories or classrooms. They show us that science is all around us; it's at the dark and frigid bottom of our oceans, it's inside an atom, it's light-years away in a galaxy we've yet to discover. My goal—and that of this series—is to travel along with people who are pursuing the seemingly impossible, journeying into the unknown. We want to be there as scientists and innovators make their discoveries. And we want you to be part of the process of discovery as well.

Accompanying these bold and courageous individuals—and documenting their work—has not been a simple task. When Mike Madden finally made his breakthrough, I—and the New Explorers camera crew—was there in the water with him. Over the years, I have also climbed into eagles' nests, tracked a deadly virus, cut my way through thick South American rain forests, trekked deep into East Africa's Masai territory, and flown jet fighters high above the clouds with some of the U.S. Air Force's most fearless Top Guns.

As you witness the achievements we bring you through New Explorers books, you may start thinking that most of the world's great discoveries have already been made, that all the great frontiers have already been explored. But nothing could be further from the truth. In fact, scientists and researchers are now uncovering more uncharted frontiers than ever before.

As host and executive producer of our television program, my mission is to find the most fascinating and exciting New Explorers of our time. I hope that their adventures will inspire you to undertake adventures of your own—to seek out and be curious, to find answers and contemplate or create solutions. At the very best, these stories will turn you into one of the world's Newest Explorers—the men and women who will capture our imaginations and thrill us with discoveries well into the 21st century.

Bill Kurtis

Bill Kurtis

South America

Rain Forest

The Amazonian rain forest is a mysterious place. Some scientists believe there are cures here for every known disease— cures that could be drawn from plants that we don't even know exist.

Hello, I'm Bill Kurtis. There are only a few people who know the secrets locked inside the green world of the rain forest. They are forest people, still living only a step away from the Stone Age. In some ways, they are more advanced than we are. Their knowledge of the rain forest provides them with food and shelter and with medicine from plants that cure their infections and heal their wounds.

The forest people use everything to survive. Cane as light as air goes into their arrows. Each arrow is tipped with feathers on one end to guide the shaft to its target. At the other end is a point for killing—a large sharp point for big game, a smaller one for birds, and a special point that is tipped with the potent curare poison. The poison is so deadly that the Indian hunters don't dare risk even scratching themselves with a treated point. Several poisonous plants are mixed together to make it.

If forest people can mix as many as 12 different plants to make deadly curare, what other secrets do they know about the plants of the rain forest? Why not ask these people which plants work best in solving the mysteries of disease? It seems simple—but it means traveling deep into the rain forest, risking danger and tropical diseases. And it means racing against time, because the rain forest is being destroyed. More than 70 million acres have already been cut down in Brazil alone.

A new group of scientists called ethnobotanists have taken up the mission of learning the medical uses of rain forest plants. They believe that their work will save, not only these valuable habitats, but perhaps the rest of the world as well. On this NEW EXPLORERS journey, we'll join one of them on a trek deep into the Amazonian rain forest, on a quest to unlock the mysteries it holds.

Suriname still holds untouched and unexplored rain forest.

An Untouched World

To reach our new explorer, we fly over some of the finest
untouched rain forest in the world, in southern Suriname (for-
merly Dutch Guyana), South America. This is just a small part
of the huge forest that covers the Amazon River basin, stretch-
ing deep into the heart of the continent. In two and a half
hours, we don't see a single road below our plane. The scene
hasn't changed for millions of years. That's why there are so
many different species of plants here—little has interrupted
the natural cycle of evolution.

The Amazon River runs through the heart of South America's lush rain forest.

CLIMATE CONTROL

Rain forests are the richest and most varied habitat on earth. They are also crucial to our planet's environmental health. Rain forest plants produce a large amount of the oxygen in the earth's atmosphere. They also take in an enormous amount of harmful carbon dioxide. (The process of photosynthesis, by which a plant makes food from sunlight, uses carbon dioxide and releases oxygen as a byproduct.)

As rain forests are lost, there are fewer plants absorbing carbon dioxide from the atmosphere. There are also fewer plants releasing oxygen. Scientists are still uncertain about the exact effects of plant loss on our atmosphere but most agree that a buildup of carbon dioxide plays a key role in a trend called global warming. If global warming continues, the average temperature of the earth will slowly rise. This will change climates and will eventually kill off untold species of plants and animals.

At last we see our destination: the village of Kwamalasamoetoe. (The name means "bamboo stand," for a stand of bamboo that grows along the riverbank here.) We were told that most planes would not land at the village. Now, a little late, we find out why. The dirt landing strip runs over the top of a hill, and the pilot has to drop down on it without catching the trees. We land safely, and our plane is met by Dr. Mark Plotkin, an American ethnobotanist. He has been here for more than a month, living with the Indians to learn which rain forest plants they use for medicine.

The village is in a remarkably beautiful setting that resembles the garden of Eden. As director of plant conservation for an international organization that sponsors scientific research, Mark Plotkin has been visiting this village for 10 years. He has a comfortable relationship with the villagers now, but it didn't start that way.

Mark explains that when he first began, he asked a local bush pilot to take him to the village closest to the Brazilian border, and the pilot dropped him here. Before he left, the pilot warned him to treat these Indian people of the forest with respect. The pilot said: "if you don't, the men will come after you, and all the arrows are tipped with poison." Mark set up a meeting with the local chiefs and explained why he had come. "They thought it was a little odd. But when they saw that I didn't mean any harm and was crazy about plants, they were very accommodating. Talking plants with these Indians is like shooting basketball with Michael Jordan."

Opposite top: Mark Plotkin takes samples of a mushroom the Tirio Indians use to fight ear infections.
Opposite bottom: The rain forest is rich in plants that contain great potential for healing. Here, Plotkin inspects a plant that yields a kind of guava berry.

LEARNING FROM THE SHAMAN

The science of ethnobotany is all about gaining the trust of people who have learned from centuries of trial and error which plants have healing powers. Such scientists hope to put the forest people's knowledge to use in modern medicine. The village shaman is the man who will lead the way for Mark. The highly knowledgeable shaman talks about the different plants we'll be looking for, and explains how these plants are used as cures.

Mark Plotkin has learned much from listening to the secrets of the rain forest shamans.

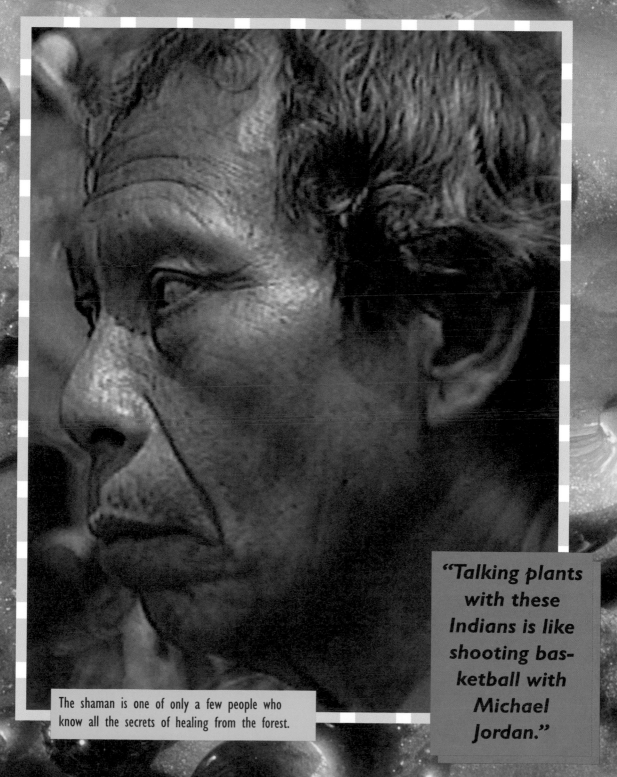

The shaman is one of only a few people who know all the secrets of healing from the forest.

"Talking plants with these Indians is like shooting bas-ketball with Michael Jordan."

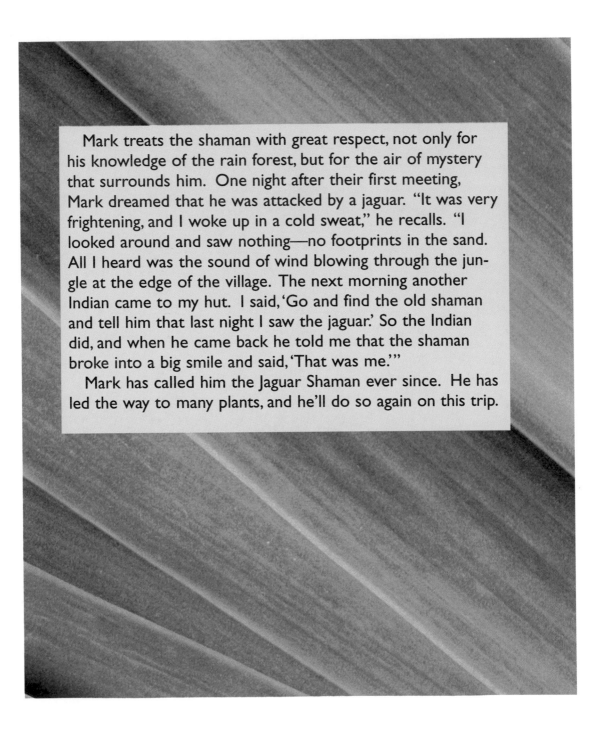

Mark treats the shaman with great respect, not only for his knowledge of the rain forest, but for the air of mystery that surrounds him. One night after their first meeting, Mark dreamed that he was attacked by a jaguar. "It was very frightening, and I woke up in a cold sweat," he recalls. "I looked around and saw nothing—no footprints in the sand. All I heard was the sound of wind blowing through the jungle at the edge of the village. The next morning another Indian came to my hut. I said, 'Go and find the old shaman and tell him that last night I saw the jaguar.' So the Indian did, and when he came back he told me that the shaman broke into a big smile and said, 'That was me.'"

Mark has called him the Jaguar Shaman ever since. He has led the way to many plants, and he'll do so again on this trip.

Mark is fascinated: The plant is a member of the ginger family, and the ancient Chinese used ginger to treat coughs and colds.

Soon we find more plants. One is used in cases of difficult childbirth. Women make a tea from the leaves, which is rubbed on the skin and drunk during the delivery. What effect does it have? Mark isn't sure. "It could be pain relief, or it could induce contractions," he says. He'll collect samples of this and other plants for analysis back in his laboratory in the United States.

Then another plant catches Mark's attention. The stem of this palm can stop bleeding. "If you're out cutting trails and you cut yourself, and the bleeding doesn't stop, here's what you do. You take this palm, crush the stem, and drip the plant juices into the wound to stop the blood flow," Mark explains. "In ethnobotanical terms, we would call it a hemostatic—that is, it stops the flow of blood."

After just a day in the village, we're beginning to appreciate what it takes to be a good ethnobotanist. To find the plants used by the Indians, you first have to convince them to show you. Then you have to ask them to teach you. That requires trust. Ten years ago, the people in this village had never met anyone like Mark Plotkin—someone who wanted to learn from them instead of telling them that Western civilization is much better. Mark says, "When you're dealing with people who might make fire by rubbing two sticks together, some would say that in many ways they're certainly more primitive than our culture. But when you're in the forest with these guys, you realize who the primitive ones are—us."

THE VANISHING RAIN FORESTS

Roughly 70 to 80 million acres (32 million hectares) of rain forest are cleared and destroyed each year.

Tropical rain forests grow in a band along the equator, where temperatures are warm year-round and rainfall is abundant. The rain forests contain the greatest variety of living things of any habitat on earth. Though they cover only 6 percent of the earth's land, about two thirds of the world's plant and animal species are found in rain forests. And scientists believe that the rain forests may contain countless undiscovered species. Thousands of species of brilliantly colored tropical birds, bats, butterflies, frogs, insects, monkeys, sloths, and snakes are among the rain forest's animals. Many species live out their lives almost entirely in the forest canopy, in trees that tower up to 200 feet (61 meters) above the ground. So do some unusual plants—dramatic orchids, mosses, ferns, and bromeliads grow on thickly covered tree limbs, drawing moisture and nutrients from the air.

Today, however, the forests are under assault. People are clearing the land for agriculture and are cutting forest trees for timber or fuel. An area of tropical rain forest roughly the size of Pennsylvania disappears every year. This situation has prompted international concern and campaigns to save the forests. But the pressure to clear the land is also strong.

Most rain forests are located in developing countries, where populations are growing, and many of the people are poor. If they can't clear land for farming or harvest timber, how will they live? Some countries are working to find ways to produce crops from the forest itself—a variety of nuts, oil from oil palms, and timber from fast-growing trees that can be replanted. Cultivating plants that yield medicines also holds promise. But so far, these efforts have not been enough to stop the destruction of the forests.

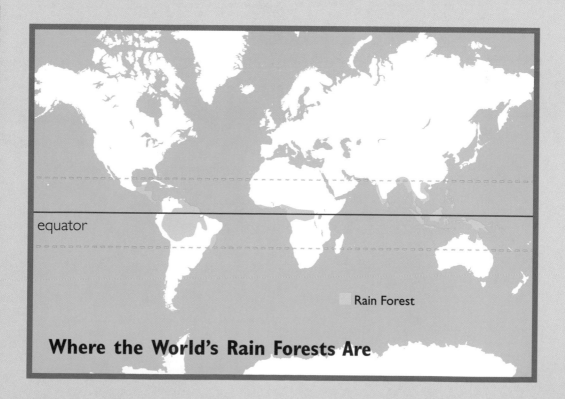

equator

Rain Forest

Where the World's Rain Forests Are

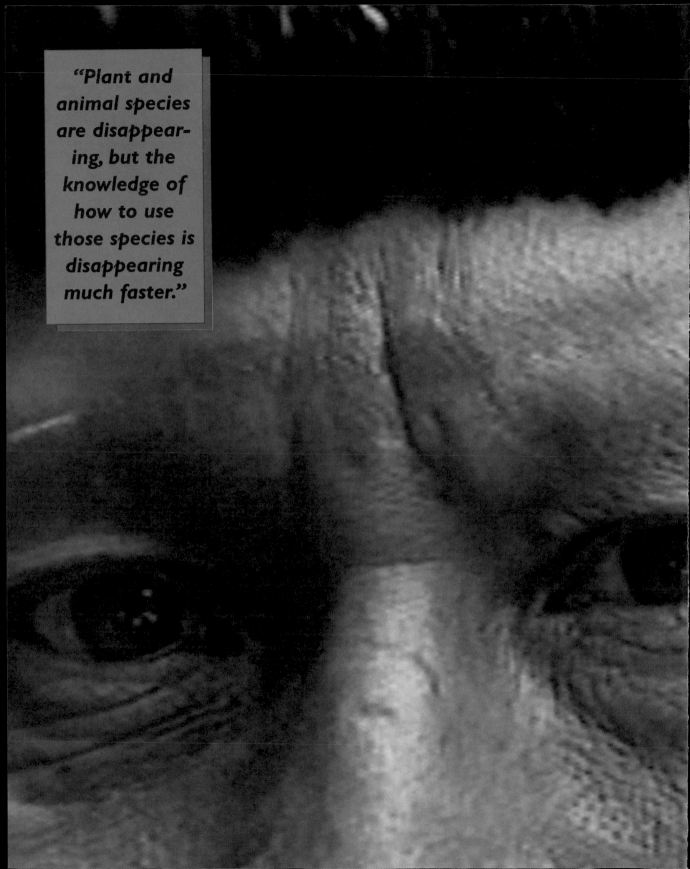

"*Plant and animal species are disappearing, but the knowledge of how to use those species is disappearing much faster.*"

Today, tropical forest peoples are disappearing around the world, absorbed by other cultures or simply dying out, says Mark. And he's in a race against time to record their knowledge. "Plant and animal species are disappearing, but the knowledge of how to use those species is disappearing much faster. When the grandsons of my friends here are all running around in coats and ties 20 years from now, they're not going to be much more knowledgeable about the forest than we are."

Over 90 Amazonian tribes have disappeared since the turn of the century. Now many remaining tribes live together in villages like this one, where the Tiríos live with the Waiwai and several other tribes. Together, they combine their knowledge of the plants of the rain forest.

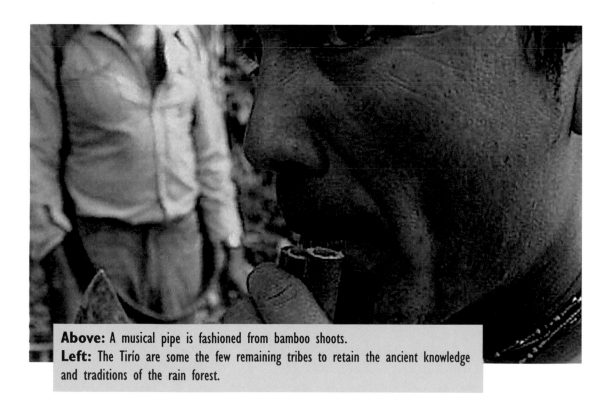

Above: A musical pipe is fashioned from bamboo shoots.
Left: The Tirío are some the few remaining tribes to retain the ancient knowledge and traditions of the rain forest.

MARK PLOTKIN:
JUNGLE EXPLORER

"I'm not a person who finds plants fascinating," says ethnobotanist Mark Plotkin. *"I just fell in love with the science. As a kid, I grew up reading books about jungle explorers. Now I come into these places, and the Indians come out of the jungle and embrace me with bear hugs—well, that's the dream of every little boy who grows up wanting to be a jungle explorer."*

Mark has learned much from the Indians over the years, but he has also contributed to their lives. On one visit, he was able to give the Tiríos a 300-page manuscript about the plant medicines used by their tribe. "The chief was so pleased that he summoned the Indians to a council in the forest the next day. He said, 'This is important stuff,' and he appointed Koita to be a sort of sorcerer's apprentice. Koita is responsible for learning this, working with me to translate it into the Tiríos' language. It will be used in the schools in the village, to teach the kids so the knowledge will be passed on."

The Tiríos are not the only forest people who have shared their secrets with Mark. He has spent time with tribes in other part of South America as well. He wrote about his adventures in a popular book, Tales of a Shaman's Apprentice: An Ethnobotanist Searches for New Medicine in the Amazon Rain Forest. Reading it is a bit like reading the books about jungle explorers that Mark read when he was a boy.

Arrow making is a delicate but essential craft for the forest people.

Making cassava bread

Although some of the Indians wear Western clothing, their lives have changed little over the centuries. The men hunt most of the day. The women seem to do most of the hard work, such as preparing cassava bread, the main item in their diet. We watch the delicate craft of arrow making and see the care used in twisting cotton into a thread. But as we watch these activities, we begin to feel a sadness, knowing that we're witnessing an ancient culture that is all too quickly being replaced with T-shirts and calico dresses.

For now, life in the village is fascinating for an outsider. Actually, there's only one thing we don't look forward to: drinking their favorite beverage, cassava beer. It's made by the women, who chew up the root of the cassava plant and then spit it into a gourd. The chewed root ferments into a

The rain forest is home to many thousands of spider species.

drink that smells a little like alcohol. Unfortunately, it's considered bad manners to reject offers of the drink, or to leave any in the gourd when you have finished drinking! Remembering that all the arrows in the village are poison-tipped, we drink it all, and learn firsthand about the brave things an ethnobotanist has to do for his profession.

ANACONDA TERRITORY

Early one morning, the Indians take us by canoe to another section of the rain forest. The forest is much denser there. The Indians say there are many different plants—and a giant snake, the anaconda. This huge relative of the boa constrictor can grow as long as 40 feet (12 meters).

Mark is undaunted by the possibility of coming upon the snake. He's in search of the virola, a tree that has blood-red sap. The Indians say this sap cures infections, skin rashes, and other diseases. In the same part of the forest, Mark also hopes to find a fungus that he believes is the forest people's answer to Western medicine's antibiotics. The Indians, too, are excited to visit this part of the forest. They're looking forward to doing some hunting while we're here.

We get ashore and begin to push into the jungle. It's another long hike, through thick vegetation and swampy ground.

The blood-red sap of the virola is used to treat skin rashes and infections.

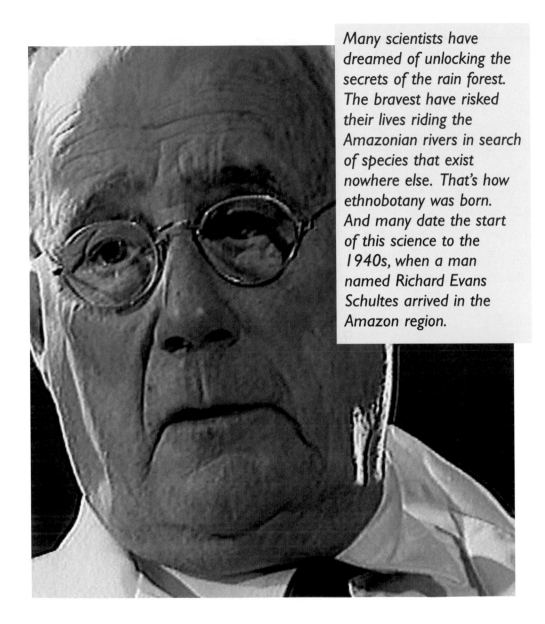

Many scientists have dreamed of unlocking the secrets of the rain forest. The bravest have risked their lives riding the Amazonian rivers in search of species that exist nowhere else. That's how ethnobotany was born. And many date the start of this science to the 1940s, when a man named Richard Evans Schultes arrived in the Amazon region.

Schultes came to study the arrow poison curare, and he ended up spending 14 years in the jungle. Altogether, he collected 24,000 species in the Amazon. He was the first to take folk medicine seriously. He discovered a mushroom in Mexico that was developed into a beta-blocker, a drug used to treat heart disease and high blood pressure. And his experiments with hallucinogens from jungle plants helped scientists blaze new frontiers in studying the mind.

Now a retired professor at Harvard University, Schultes is considered one of the great conservationists of his time. He also earned a reputation as a teacher who could fire the imagination of his students—sometimes by demonstrating his skill with a South American blowgun. On a good day, he can nail a bull's-eye across the room.

Schultes says he has always stressed the importance of field work for his students, telling them they would need at least a year of it. "You've got to go down to the Amazon, or the Andes, or wherever, and know these plants as they're growing," he says. "You collect them, naturally, but you've got to know them as living things."

Finally, the Jaguar Shaman leads Mark to the tree with the blood-red sap that he has been looking for. When a piece of bark is slit off, reddish plant resin oozes out.

Mark explains that the plant is a type of wild nutmeg. The Indians use it for several purposes, he says, but the most important use is to clear up fungal infections. He has more than just their stories to vouch for the effects of the resin: "I've used it on myself, and it works," he says. "Professor Schultes, from Harvard, has found Indians in the Colombian Amazon using it to treat infections of the skin. And Indians in Venezuela have used it against fungal infections of the skin. So here you have widely separated Indian tribes using the plant

Left and above: The Tirió know how to utilize almost everything in the forest. Here, they weave drinking cups and backpacks from palm leaves they have collected.

The forest provides everything for these people.

Rubbed along a machete blade, a leaf becomes a bird caller.

for the same purpose. And that would indicate to me that there's something to it."

While we've been searching for the virola, the Indians have been busy. After all, this tall forest is their "department store," their "grocery," and their "pharmacy." Their skills are impressive: With a few slits and folds, a palm leaf becomes a drinking cup. Another leaf, cut and rubbed on the blade of a machete, becomes a bird caller. A rest break gives the forest people enough time to weave a backpack from plant materials and cut wood from the buttress root of a tree. They'll carve the wood into a paddle for the trip back up the river.

The forest provides everything—entertainment, clothes, medicine, and, of course, food. Wuta, the hunter, is busy searching for unsuspecting birds and monkeys in the trees, and for peccaries (wild pigs) in the forest underbrush. He increases his chances of returning home with food by tipping his arrows with his deadly curare. The poison lasts for months, if not years, and kills anything it hits. There are different types of curare, and most interfere with the ability to breathe. Victims, who basically suffocate, face an agonizing death.

Bill Kurtis and Mark Plotkin watch as sap oozes out of the highly prized Virola tree.

Plants as Medicine

Plants have been an important source of medicines in all cultures, going back to ancient times. Today scientists have identified at least 20,000 useful plants, and many of them grow in the tropical rain forest. In fact, one of every four medicines contains natural material, and about half of those contain plant matter. Here are just some of the miracle drugs that have been developed from plants.

- The opium poppy, from Asia, is made into the painkiller morphine.
- The plant extracts used in the arrow poison curare are turned into tubocurarine, a muscle relaxant used during abdominal surgery.

Rosy periwinkle

- The rosy periwinkle, from Madagascar, is the source of vincristine, used in chemotherapy for childhood leukemia, and vinblastine, used to fight Hodgkin's disease.
- Reserpine, traditionally used in India for snakebite, helps reduce blood pressure.
- Ephedrine, from China, is used to treat asthma, hay fever, and low blood pressure.
- The purple foxglove is the source of

digitalis, used to treat heart disease.
- The South American cinchona tree is used to produce quinine, which cures malaria.

These medicines are powerful drugs—in fact, like curare, many plant extracts can be deadly. But in the right formulas, and the right amount, they can also heal.

Today many drug companies are reluctant to look to plants for new medicines because so many drugs can be made artificially, in the laboratory. But the National Cancer Institute

Purple foxglove

Cinchona

(NCI) has taken a different stance. At its research center in Frederick, Maryland, the NCI has started a $50 million project to find natural products that might help in the fight against cancer and acquired immunodeficiency syndrome (AIDS).

The research is promising, but there's an urgency to the NCI's mission. Deforestation—the rapid clearing of the world's rain forests—won't stand still while scientists investigate the various medical promises of rain forest plants.

One of the first Europeans to visit the Amazon region, the British adventurer Sir Walter Raleigh, saw for himself curare's terrible effects. He sailed up the Orinoco River in search of El Dorado, a legendary city of gold. His son was hit by a poison arrow and died a horrible death on their ship. White men have been interested in finding an antidote to the poison ever since.

Mark shows us a plant that the Indians use. "If they're out hunting and the arrow hits them accidentally, they use this," he says. "A number of tribes have different antidotes. The ones that have been tested so far haven't been effective. As far as I know, this one hasn't been tested in the laboratory." But the Indians say it works. And here in the forest, what they know is as good as any proven laboratory test.

The Jaguar Shaman has gone ahead, and now he returns to tell Mark that he has found something special. It's the fungus that Mark has been looking for: a flat, mushroom-like growth sprouting from a rotting log on the forest floor. The Indians call this ivory-colored fungus golobe. They explain how to use it: Squeeze the sap out of the fungus and drip it into aching ears to cure an earache. Mark is excited—infection-fighting drugs have been developed from fungi related to this one, but this species has never been looked at. Perhaps it will yield a new drug to use against a disease that has so far proved untreatable.

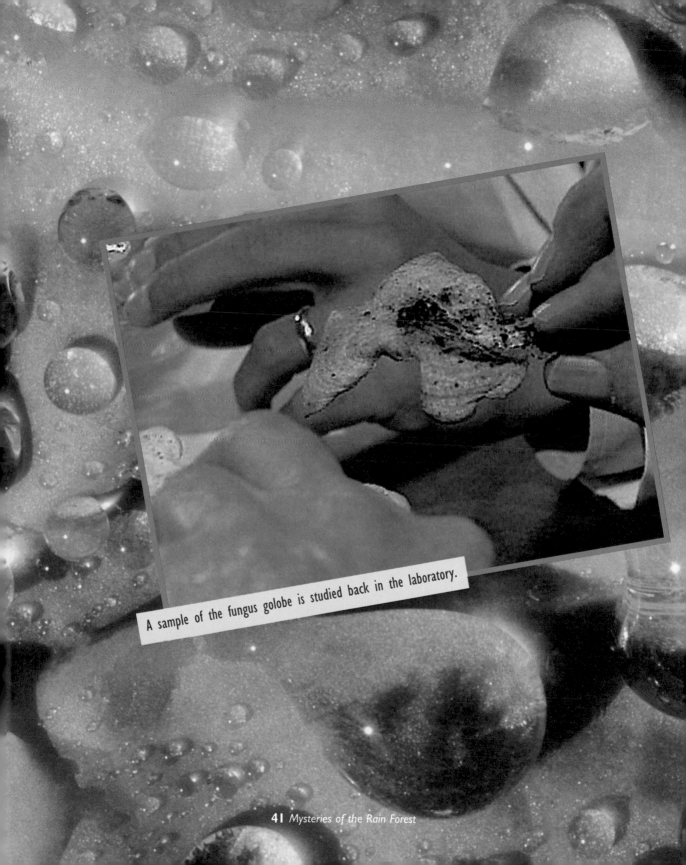

A sample of the fungus golobe is studied back in the laboratory.

DEFORESTATION FACTS

The world's rain forests are being destroyed at an alarming rate. Following are some statistics complied by two environmental organizations.

• According to the Rain Forest Action Network, about 78 million acres (31 million hectares) of rain forest are destroyed each year. That is an area larger than Poland. This translates to roughly 214,000 acres (86,000 hectares) per day (an area larger than New York City); 150 acres (60 hectares) per minute; and 2.47 acres (1 hectare) per second (roughly the size of two U.S. football fields).

• The Rain Forest Action Network also estimates that roughly 50,000 species of living things are driven into extinction each year. This translates to 137 species each day.

• The World Wildlife Fund estimates that, at the current rate of rain forest destruction, all the forests will be gone by 2050. Some countries, such as Ivory Coast, Nigeria, Costa Rica, and Sri Lanka are likely to lose all their rain forest as early as 2010 if no conservation steps are taken.

HOME TO THE LAB

On this journey to the rain forest of Suriname, Mark found what he was looking for, and so did we. Nearly a week of plant hunting has helped us learn about the rain forest and the people who live there. But now it's time to say good-bye and begin the long journey home. Luckily, we will be weighed down carrying rare plants from the Amazon. The village marks our departure with a traditional dance.

For Mark, leaving Kwamalasamoetoe is the most difficult part of the journey. For him, the village and its surrounding forest is a magical place. But his work is as important outside the rain forest as within it. He'll return to his office in Washington, D.C., to analyze what he has found. Before he does, however, there is one more important leg to this journey. He will go back to the Harvard Botanical Museum to see his former professor Richard Schultes— the one man who will most appreciate what he has found.

Medical laboratories in the United States analyze the properties of plant samples taken from the rain forest.

Constant testing and analysis are needed to unlock the medial potential of new plant species.

Of all the students who have followed Schultes' advice and set out to learn from the tribes of the world, the one who has followed most closely in his footsteps is Mark Plotkin. Mark has made ethnobotany in the Amazon his life's work.

In many ways, Mark Plotkin and Richard Schultes are both medicine men, born, perhaps, in the wrong time and place. Despite their clothes and university degrees, their spirits are closest to another place and another tribe—to the Amazon and its promise of the unknown.

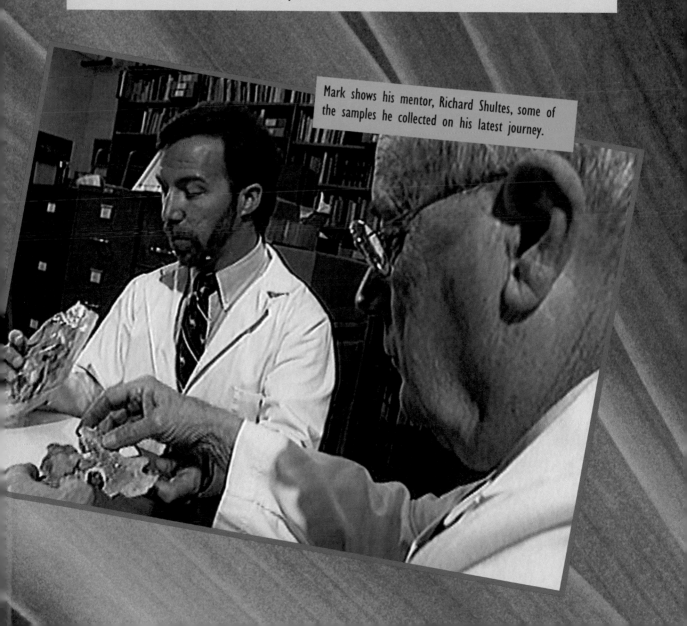

Mark shows his mentor, Richard Shultes, some of the samples he collected on his latest journey.

GLOSSARY

antidote A drug that halts or reverses the effects of a poison.

bromeliad A family of plants, including the pineapple, that usually grow on other plants.

buttress root A wide root that flares out from the trunk of a tree and reaches the ground, helping to support the tree.

cassava A plant with a starchy root, native to the Amazon region and widely grown for food there.

ethnobotanist A scientist who studies the plant lore of different peoples

fungus A group of plants that includes mushrooms.

gourd A fruit with a hard rind that is used as a bowl.

hallucinogen A drug that alters perceptions, producing visions and delusions.

hemostatic Something that stops the flow of blood.

resin A gummy fluid produced by certain plants.

shaman A healer believed to have magical powers, who uses plants and spells to cure the sick and commune with the spirit world.

species A group of plants.

FURTHER READING

Gallant, Roy A. *Earth's Vanishing Forests*. New York: Macmillan, 1991.

Goodman, Billy. *The Rain Forest*. New York: Little, Brown, 1991.

Lewington, Anna. *Rain Forest Amerindians*. Chatham, NJ: Raintree Steck-Vaughn, 1993.

Liptak, Karen. *Endangered Peoples*. New York: Franklin Watts, 1993.

Nichol, John. *The Mighty Rainforest*. New York: Sterling, 1990.

Plotkin, Mark J. *Tales of a Shaman's Apprentice: An Ethnobotanist Searches for New Medicine in the Amazon Rain Forest*. New York: Viking, 1993.

Reading, Susan. *Plants of the Tropics*. New York: Facts on File, 1990.

Sayre, April Pulley. *Tropical Rain Forest*. New York: Twenty-First Century, 1994.

Web Sites

http://www.pbs.org/wttw/web_newexp/
The official homepage of The New Explorers television series. Lists the show broadcast schedule, educational resources, and information about how to join The New Explorers Club as well as how to participate in The New Explorers electronic field trip.

http://outcast.gene.com/ae/WN/NM/plotkin1.html
An interview with Mark Plotkin, Ph.d., Executive Director, Ethnobiology and Conservation Team, and author of "Tales of the Shaman's Apprentice."

http://www.ran.org/ran/
Take a look at the rainforest through images, video, art, and question and answer pages.

http://outcast.gene.com/ae/RC/Ethnobotany/index.html
General background information on the science of Ethnobotany, featuring a section of suggested classroom activities and experiments.

http://www.rainforest-alliance.org/
An international nonprofit organization dedicated to tropical forest conservation. Interactive jungle adventure. Special resources for teachers, kids, and conservationists.

http://www.conservation.org/web/aboutci/strategy/shaman.htm
Information about what Conservation International is doing to help preserve the Tirio tribe's knowledge of medicinal plants and other rainforest products.

http://www.mhtc.net/~saverft/
Save The Rainforest, a nonprofit organization that specializes in conducting rainforest tours and courses for teachers and students. Also produces rainforest curriculums, videos, posters, and involves schools in conservation projects in the tropics.

Index

Photo Credits

Page 3: Bill Arnold
Page 42: Will Crockett
All other photographic images: © Kurtis Productions Ltd. and WTTW/Chicago
Map: © Blackbirch Press, Inc.